MANA

Administrate

LEADERS
Provide Vision

COACHES

Deliver Results!!

COACHING 2 WIN!

A Guide To Help Managers Deliver Results

CHICK WADDELL

To order additional copies of

COACHING TO WIN

complete the Order Form found on the last page of this book.

For information on Excellence in Action Partners
products and services

call 1-888-505-9052

visit www.chickwaddell.com

Printed in the United States of America
ISBN: 0-966939719

Book design: Defae Weaver
Cover design: Mike McCormick

STEPS TO GET THE MOST OUT OF THIS BOOK!

+ Read with a highlighter in your hand. Highlight key words or phrases that relate to your management situation.

+ Complete the Coaches Evaluation at the end of this book.

+ When you complete this book, order additional copies for those who manage others.

LET THE GAME BEGIN!!

COACHING IS ABOUT:

1. Creating an **empowered organization** where everyone takes ownership of the mission.

2. Developing people by "problem giving" as much as "problem solving" and by challenging employees to **think and grow on their own**.

3. Communicating the idea that **everyone** ultimately **serves** or sells **the customer**.

4. Providing the ideas, the support, the know-how and the tools to **help subordinates succeed.** Managers succeed only when the team succeeds.

5. Hiring people with the attitude and the aptitude to **get the job done**.

6. Understanding that employees are **motivated for their reasons, not yours.**

COACHING IS ABOUT:

7. Evaluation and measurement and about assessing, how far you've come, and effectively **forecasting where you are going.**

8. Communicating the reality that **failure isn't fatal,** but often a stepping stone to higher achievement.

9. The fact that we don't manage time, **we manage ourselves within chunks of time.**

10. The insight that for motivation to be **effective** it must be meaningful to the person being motivated.

11. Helping the employee to **think like an owner** by giving them decision making equity.

12. Developing a team that will **function effectively** in the manager's absence.

CONTENTS

-1-
FUNDAMENTALS
OF COACHING

> **"You don't change culture; you coach people to WIN."**
> Lawrence Bossidy
> CEO
> Allied Signal Corp.

"This city with all its houses, palaces, steam engines, cathedrals and huge immeasurable traffic and tumult, what is it but thought, but millions of Thoughts made into one — a huge immeasurable Spirit of Thought embodied in brick, in iron, in smoke, dust, palaces, parliaments, coaches, docks and the rest of it! Not a brick was made but someone had to think of the making of that brick."
Thomas Carlyle

Whether it be the Panama Canal, the Transcontinental Railroad, the great cities of our age or the space station being built today, nothing gets accomplished without the work and creative power of people. All great organizations and companies possess one common denominator: *productive people.*

It doesn't matter what business you're in; if you're in a management position, you're in the people business first. Organizations fail because managers fail. Managers fail because they fail to coach their people.

> *Organizations fail because managers fail. Managers fail because they fail to coach their people.*

Webster defines coaching as *to train or instruct*. While this is true it's much more than that. Coaching is the skill of attaining results by developing people to their maximum ability.

It's an improvement on the old proverb —

> *Tell me and I will remember*
>
> *Teach me and I'll learn*
>
> *Involve me and I will act*

Let's add —

> *Coach me and I will improve.*

The task is to get everyone thinking, acting and moving forward together toward a common goal.

Effective coaches wear two hats:

- **MANAGEMENT HAT**
- **LEADERSHIP HAT**

They wear the *management* hat to provide for the continuation of the business. It might involve administrative nuts and bolts like overseeing policy/procedures, employee compensation, EEOC and more.

They wear the *leadership* hat to provide vision and to lead others to lead themselves.

They manage to keep the business running effectively. They lead providing vision to light the path to adapt to change. They coach developing people who deliver results.

PRODUCTION PYRAMID

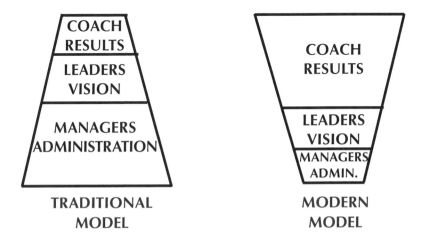

TRADITIONAL MODEL

MODERN MODEL

Coaching calls for the development of new skills that take the spotlight away from simply managing numbers and statistics to building the organization's most critical resource — **PEOPLE**. With people as the focus, these keys are fundamental to coaching success. To be a winning coach, you must be:

P — Philosophy focused

E — Establish standards

O — Objective driven

P — Paradigm shifting

L — Let them know you care

E — Encourage and build belief

> *Although strategies are important they don't grow the organization, people implementing strategies grow organizations.*

Modern day managers initiate business strategies, quality strategies, and sales/marketing strategies with the expectation that each will play their part in successfully driving their business forward. Although strategies are important they don't grow the organization, people implementing strategies grow organizations.

P – PHILOSOPHY FOCUSED

Your philosophy of coaching begins with your core beliefs and values.

> *"Everything I do is to prepare people to perform at the best of their abilities. These beliefs drive my entire philosophy of coaching. My coaching beliefs in a nutshell are:*
>   1. *Keep winning and losing in perspective*
>   2. *Teach by example*
>   3. *Go for respect over popularity*
>   4. *Value character as well as ability*
>   5. *Work hard but enjoy what you do."*
>
>   Don Shula
>   *Everyone's A Coach*

Whether you are coaching a company, a football team or a business team, your philosophy, values and beliefs are the foundation to your present and future success.

E – ESTABLISH STANDARDS

> *"Winning isn't a sometime thing. It's an all the time thing."*
>
>   Vince Lombardi

For those who may not have heard of Lombardi, he is a coaching legend, and his success wasn't by accident. As coach, he set the expectation and standards of performance for the team and for each player. It is said that he started each new season by asking every team member to bring their wrist watches to practice. He would then ask that everyone set their watch ten minutes ahead. The new standard time would be "Lombardi time." When the rest of the world was on time, his team would be ten minutes early.

> **P**erformance standards are based on the position, not the person. They are met when the job has been performed in an acceptable manner.

In addition to time standards, many other types of standards exist. There are standards of dress, standards of conduct and standards of performance. Performance standards are based on the position, not the person. They are met when the job has been performed in an acceptable manner. We want to know if subordinates can perform the tasks and possess the knowledge and skills to do the job. Standards of performance are created first to guide behavior and second to establish a basis upon which effectiveness can be measured.

O – OBJECTIVE DRIVEN

Successful organizations are objective driven and the main objective of the team is to help fulfill the company mission. The mission communicates where the organization is going and the route it will take to get there. It should detail the purpose and beliefs of the organization. The mission is the guidepost of the entire organization and it should not just hang on the wall. To be effective, it must be communicated to all. The mission is effective only when it becomes a reality in the minds and actions of everyone working in the organization. The everyday challenge of management is to create an empowered organization where everyone takes ownership of the mission.

The challenge of the coach is to help each person understand what part they play in fulfilling it and then get them to do it.

> *The mission is effective only when it becomes a reality in the minds and actions of everyone working in the organization.*

P – PARADIGM SHIFTING

I know some of you think this is a backfield shift designed by Coach Knute Rockne of Notre Dame back in the late 1920's. Yes and no. *A paradigm shift is a new way of thinking about an old problem.* As a creative thinker, Rockne was one of the first to use the forward pass in a football game and he was always creating new strategies and tactics for victory. In addition to coaching for Notre Dame, Rockne also taught chemistry at the university. My high school chemistry teacher called chemistry "cooking." Rockne was always cooking up something new and creative. Another creative thinker, Marcel Proust, author of the classic "Remembrance of Things Past" summarized it all when he said *"the real voyage of discovery consists not in seeing new lands but in seeing with new eyes."* Today we call that type of thinking, thinking outside of the box.

A golfing buddy related a great example:

> A golfer is standing at a beautiful par five hole at the St. Simons Island Golf Club. He hits a perfect approach shot. As the golfer walks up over a knoll in front of the green, he can't find the ball. After further search-

ing, he sees the ball has rolled into a paper bag on the side of the green. So what does he do?

Number 1: Take a stroke and remove the ball from the bag.
Number 2: Give it a good, old-fashioned whack.
Number 3: Wait and hope the wind blows the bag away from the ball.

None of the above!

Instead he takes out a match and burns the bag. He's an outside the box thinker.

The new paradigm for management is to effectively communicate that everyone, no matter what they do, ultimately sells or serves the external customer. Employees either sell or serve the end customer or they serve the people that do. The people on the front line take care of the end customer and it's everyone else's job to take care of the front line people. Everyone must deliver value to the customer through their words and through their actions.

> *The people on the front line take care of the end customer and it's everyone else's job to take care of the front line people.*

Managers who coach think outside the box. They possess the ability to successfully adapt to the change and aren't afraid to take the road less traveled.

L - LET THEM KNOW YOU CARE

People don't care how much you know until they know how much you care about them. If ever there was a secret to coaching success, this is it.

I am saying that employees must be seen as more than just a part of a production process. Employees are people; people who want to be valued for more than their ability to show up for work and just do a job. Some time back, the human relations Hawthorne Study measured the correlation between working conditions, employee value and performance output. The significance of the study is that it showed that productivity increased regardless of conditions whenever the employee sensed they were valued members of the organization. Letting an employee know that they are valued means showing them how much you care. When coaches express that they care about the subordinate that employee often mirrors that behavior outwardly with positive communication to the customer.

> **W**hen coaches express they care about the subordinate that employee often mirrors that behavior outwardly with positive communication to the customer.

E – ENCOURAGE AND BUILD BELIEF

Zig Ziglar wasn't always a shining star in the world of selling. In the early years, he struggled like many other sales people. Then one day everything changed. His opportunity clock, as he calls it, went off early one cold winter morning. He got up, got into his car and sped off to his monthly sales meeting. Zig didn't know it, but it was the day that was going to change his life. After attending the sales meeting, the president of his company asked to speak to Ziglar. Ziglar says that if it hadn't been for those words of encouragement that day, he may have decided to start looking for another job. The company president, P. C. Merrill, said "Zig, I've been watching you and you have real ability. You are champion caliber. I'm looking at you as a future officer of this company."

Those words of belief inspired Ziglar to become the number two salesperson in the company among 7,000 individuals. Those encouraging words so transformed Ziglar's thinking about himself that they changed his life and in turn, Ziglar has touched and changed the lives of millions.

Effective coaching has everything to do with your skill and ability to impart your belief in a player's or employee's capability.

The following poem "Which Am I?" sums up much of the encouragement side of coaching.

WHICH AM I?

I watched them tearing a building down –
*   a gang of men in a busy town.*
With a ho-heave-ho and lusty yell
*   they swung a beam and a side wall fell;*
I asked the foreman, "Are these men skilled,
*   the men you'd hire if you had to build?"*
He gave a laugh and said, "No, indeed!"
*   just common labor is all I need;*
I can easily wreck in a day or two
*   what builders have taken a year to do!"*
And I thought to myself as I went away
*   "Which of these roles have I tried to play?"*
Am I a builder who works with care,
*   measuring life by the rule and square?*
Am I shaping my deed to a well made plan,
*   patiently doing the best I can?*
Or am I a wrecker, who walks the town,
*   content with the labor of tearing down?*
Which are you?

Author unknown
Jess Kenner

-2-
ONE ON ONE
COACHING

> **I**t is only as we develop others that we permanently succeed."
>
> **Harry Firestone**

Becoming an effective coach doesn't happen overnight. It is a skill and like any skill, it takes knowledge, practice and application. One on One Coaching is a process that involves two phases:

- Assessment
- Action/Implementation

ASSESSMENT

During the assessment phase of coaching, you observe and assess the subordinates' performance. The performance standard is defined as a condition that exists when the job has been performed is an acceptable manner. The standard is usually the minimum accepted performance relating to quantity of work, quality of work, effective use of time or cost effectiveness. You want to know if the subordinate is performing the right tasks and if they have developed the skills to effectively do the job. You ask yourself questions like:

1. If the subordinate's performance is poor, how much time and effort do you feel it will take to improve the sub-par performance? Is it worth it?
2. Does the subordinate realize the performance is below expectations? Don't assume the subordinate understands what you expect.
3. Does the subordinate understand the details of doing the job? To crystallize what's expected every subordinate should be given a written job description detailing roles, responsibilities and tasks to be completed.
4. Does the subordinate know how to do the job? Has there been adequate training relating to product knowledge and communication? Remember, just because the subordinate has passed a knowledge test it doesn't mean they are trained. If a person passes a test that means they are educated on a specific topic, product or issue. Training relates to developing skills and being able to practically apply knowledge in the field. Your job is to provide the support, the ideas, know-how and the tools to help the subordinate successfully accomplish the job. By the way, do your best to stay off the field of play.

> *Training relates to developing skills and being able to practically apply knowledge in the field.*

The second phase of one-on-one coaching involves action and implementation. Regularly meet with your subordinate to get and give feedback to identify ways to improve performance.

Preparation Rules:
- This is not a group exercise (This is a one-on-one session.)
- Create an environment where learning can occur
- Create a coaching objective. (This applies to both face-to-face and telephone coaching.)
- Implement the process. (Refer below.)

ACTION AND IMPLEMENTATION

A — Agree on the problem or challenge.

C — Commit to a mutual goal.

T — Teach and Train

I — Initiate an action plan.

O — Observe and give feedback.

N — Negotiate follow up.

Agree on the problem/challenge.

Why — Don't assume the employee knows a problem or challenge exists. They may not be aware of the details unless you point it out to them.

How — Ask the employee's opinion and request they evaluate their own progress. Give them responsibility and accountability as a team member.

Commit to a mutual goal.

Why —When the employee develops and commits to a mutual goal, they become the author of the commitment. They have taken ownership of the goal.

How —You have previously agreed on the challenge; now agree what should be realistically expected. Together identify skills and knowledge needed to improve.

Teach and train.

Why — Improvement often involves gaining knowledge or developing skills. Both impact performance and will help improve results.

How — Provide information and knowledge. Practice and apply the changes then create a positive consequence.

Initiate action plan.

Why — We have identified the challenge, we have set the goal. We have identified the skills and knowledge to get there. Now develop a way to make it work.

How — Refer to Action Plan Worksheet.

Observe and give feedback.

Why — Observe the plan in action. In addition, use feedback to guide and reinforce the employee. It is important to encourage and reinforce accomplishments. (Catch them doing something right.)

How — Ask if the plan is on target. If not, it may need to be adjusted. If so, be sure to mutually agree.

Negotiate follow up.

Why — Reaffirm the commitment and confirm understanding of the expectation.

How — Review the Action Plan and reconfirm dates and objectives.

Effectively implementing the One on One Action Process depends on the objective you want to accomplish and the knowledge and skill level of the person you are coaching. A coaching session might take thirty minutes or thirty seconds depending on the individual and the goal.

> *In a nutshell* **coaching** *is the every day* **pursuit** *of* **excellence.** *It's an ongoing process. The* **fact** *is we really never turn the corner* — **we're always turning the corner.** BEWARE, *the moment you think you've arrived, that's the instant* **you get left behind.**

ACTION PLAN WORKSHEET

Performance Goal:
Potential Roadblocks:
Ways to Get Around the Roadblock:
Skills, Knowledge, Relationships to Attain Goal:

ACTION STEPS	Date Completed
1. _____	_____
2. _____	_____
3. _____	_____
4. _____	_____
5. _____	_____
6. _____	_____
7. _____	_____
8. _____	_____
9. _____	_____
10. _____	_____

_____   _____
Signature   Signature

-3-
PLAYER
SELECTION

> **"I** will have no man work for me who has not the capacity to become a partner."
> **J.C. Penney**

"Your talent determines what you can do. Your motivation determines how much you are willing to do. Your attitude determines how well you will do it."

Lou Holtz, Coach
Author, *Winning Every Day*

Selecting a winner for your team means hiring someone with both the aptitude and the attitude to get the job done. Now that doesn't mean that anyone with the right mental attitude can do anything. I don't think Karl Malone, basketball great for the Utah Jazz, would make a very good jockey. Get the picture?

You need different knowledge and different skills to do different things. So when we decide to hire a new person for the team, let's begin by painting a clear picture of the employee you want to hire. Describe the job and identify the skills and qualities necessary to do the job effectively.

EXAMPLE: Job Title – Account Rep – Software Sales

Skills/Knowledge	Qualities/Characteristics
Lead generation	Trust
Qualifying customers	Discipline
Target marketing	Desire
Telephone appointment	Loyalty
Call preparation	Self confidence
Opening the call	Empathy
Questioning	Initiative
Communicating value	Positive attitude
Listening skills	Belief factor
Asking for the business	Motivation
Addressing concerns	Determination
Initiating action	
Customer service follow up	
Relationship development	
Industry knowledge	
Computer skills	
Letter writing skills	
Stand-up speaking skills	
Team selling	
Time management	
Goal setting	

Identify the job title and then prepare a list of skills, knowledge, and qualities necessary to effectively perform the job.

Job Title:_____

	Skill/Knowledge		Qualities/Characteristics
1.		1.	
2.		2.	
3.		3.	
4.		4.	
5.		5.	
6.		6.	
7.		7.	

Skills Qualities Worksheet

List in priority the specific skills and qualities you believe are essential to do the job and why.

	Skill/Knowledge	Why Important
1.		
2.		
3.		
4.		

	Qualities/Characteristics	Why Important
1.		
2.		
3.		
4.		
5.		

One of the tasks of being a coach is to describe the job in detail. This will help you to consolidate your thinking about the roles, responsibilities and tasks that must be performed for the employee to be successful.

-4-

REASONS COACHES FAIL

> **"S**uccess isn't forever! Failure isn't fatal."
> **Don Shula**

1. FAIL TO EFFECTIVELY COMMUNICATE

"Seek first to understand, then to be understood."

Steven Covey

Keys to Effective Communication:
- Seek to know your customer
- Keep the boss informed
- Keep the team informed
- Keep the lines of communication open
- Listen more than you talk
- Communicate your expectations
- Provide regular and clear feedback
- Use all delivery channels (i.e., face-to-face, fax, e-mail, phone, newsletters, memos, personal notes, small group meeting, video, video conferencing)

Design the Job

Effective communication begins with the manager painting a clear picture of what's expected from the subordinate. He designs the job by providing answers to the following questions:

1. Do you know and understand the company mission?
2. What role do you play in fulfilling the mission?
3. Who are your most important internal and external customers?
4. What are the responsibilities and tasks in effectively performing the job?
5. What are the standards of performance?

Maintain an Open and Closed Door Policy

Now that's a contradiction of words if I've ever heard one. What I mean is the door should always be open to everyone unless you decide to close it. Maybe the most destructive act a manager can do is to reprimand or embarrass an employee in front of someone else. When that happens, you have immediately lost the trust and confidence of that employee. You have set a relationship back months with one inconsiderate act. Two good rules to follow are if you reprimand do it in private behind closed doors and when you critique remember to critique the performance not the performer!

Now, although you maintain an open door policy, don't make it a revolving door where you as the manager solve all problems for all people. Steve Brown, past president of the Fortune Group Internal reminds us in his book, *Thirteen Fatal Errors Managers Make,* that we must be problem givers, not problem solvers. He says, "You should stop and listen to each employee's problem and counsel him as best you can, but no effective manager allows an employee to enter his or her office with a problem that the employee does not carry out the door upon leaving."

Being the department problem solver may be great for one's ego, but it does nothing to help develop your people. Developing people involves effectively communicating and challenging an employee to think and grow and think on their own.

> **D**eveloping people involves effectively communicating and challenging an employee to think and grow on their own.

There was a scene in the acclaimed movie, *Saving Private Ryan*, in which the hero Captain John Miller explains to one of the privates that problems go up the chain of command from privates to sergeants to lieutenants and on up the ladder. Although that may have worked in the military in 1942, it doesn't work in corporate America today. As we move through the new millennium, challenges and problems must be pushed down the line to achieve results.

2. FAIL TO BE PERSONALLY ACCOUNTABLE

The cornerstone of business growth is personal accountability. Whether the team is winning or losing, someone must be accountable for the bottom line and end

> *As we move through the new millennium, challenges and problems must be pushed down the line to achieve results.*

results. If you're in management, that person is you. It is far too easy for those in a position of power to escape taking responsibility for disappointing results. All too often, when things are not going the way we would like them to go, we make excuses and shift blame or by making comments such as:

- "I'd be more effective if I only had a bigger budget."
- "We just can't cover a region this size with so few people."
- "Operations dropped the ball. Now we're responsible for performing a miracle.
- "If we only had the right technology in place, we'd do better."

What we're really saying is, "I'm not responsible for these results and outcomes. Other people and circumstances are the reason things aren't going the way they should be going. It's not my fault!"

We should remember that when we point the finger at others, three fingers are pointing back at ourselves. In his autobiography, Lee Iacocca suggests that personal accountability is one of the keys to his success. The management system he used to turn around Chrysler Corporation all started with accountability at the very top. He asked his key people for 90 day plans and priorities. This strategy was so effective it was implemented all the way down the chain of command and Iacocca said, "On the surface, this procedure may seem like little more than a tough minded way to make employees accountable to the boss. It is that, of course, but it's also much more, because the quarterly review system makes employees accountable to themselves." Personal accountability is about making yourself accountable by asking the question, "How can I make a difference?"

> **P**ersonal account- ability is about mak- ing yourself account- able by asking the question, "How can I make a difference?"

Even though the buck stopped with Coach Iacocca, he realized everyone had to be individually responsible and accountable for Chrysler to survive and succeed. Because years have passed by we, as Paul Harvey would say, "know the rest of the story." Chrysler not only succeeded but prospered. Good job, Coach Iacocca!

3. FAIL TO DEVELOP SELF-LEADERSHIP SKILLS

Self-leadership is defined as the process of maximizing our time and talents to achieve predetermined GOALS. *Whether it's a personal goal or a professional goal we need some type of process that will take us to our destination.*

GOAL SETTING PROCESS

The goal setting process is a pragmatic tool that can link personal wants and corporate goals. Often what we want of the job can be attained through high achievement on the job.

STEP I – GOALS

Decide what you want to be, do, or have. (Describe it in writing and in detail.)

Example (List priority to the left):

A₁ ___ 1. Lose ___ pounds by _____ (date).

_____ 2. Complete my new book by _____(date).

_____ 3. Retire by age _____ with an income of _____.

_____ 4. Rollerblade across America

Make sure your goals are congruent with your values (i.e., honesty, integrity, character). Prioritize the goals A_1, A_2, A_3, A_4.

STEP 2 – Determine Objectives (Baby Goals)
Example: A_1 – Lose _____ pounds by _____ date

1. Determine a diet that I will stick to.

2. Identify a practical exercise regime that I will do.

3. Establish a daily time table that works.

STEP 3 – Identify Tasks (Convert objectives into action tasks with completion dates)

Objective 1: *Determine diet I will stick to.*

Tasks:

1. Refer to my doctor for health status, update, and diet recommendation. See doctor by _____ (date).

2. Determine what to eat and start diet on _____(date).

3. Set weight loss objective for first two weeks. Then reset the goal.

    2 week objective: _____ pounds by _____ (date).

Objective 2: *Identify a practical exercise regime that I will do.*

Tasks:

1. Rollerblade every morning for 20 minutes.

   Start date _____.

2. Do isorobics for 10 minutes every day.

   Start date _____.

3. Work on strength endurance and flexibility exercises for a total of ten minutes every morning.

   Start date _____.

Objective 3: *Get plenty of rest and sleep.*

Tasks:

1. Lights out no later than 11:00 pm.

2. Sleep in on Saturday morning.

3. Promise myself to take at least 3 mini vacations a year.

   Vacation dates: _____, _____, _____.

The reality of goal setting is that the plan rarely works exactly as it is originally written. You will have to regularly shape and mold the plan. Case in point: The astronauts on their journey to the moon had to repeatedly readjust their flight trajectory to stay on course to get to their goal.

> *The reality of goal setting is that the plan rarely works exactly as it is originally written. You will have to regularly shape and mold the plan.*

4. FAIL TO TEACH AND TRAIN

The bonsai tree, grown in Japan is unique because its height is measured in inches, not feet. Northern California has the famous giant Sequoia trees. One of these Sequoia trees is nicknamed "General Sherman" and it measures 272 feet in height and 72 feet in diameter. It is estimated that if General Sherman were cut down, it would build 35 five-bedroom homes.

Both the bonsai tree and General Sherman had the same beginning. At one time, as seeds, they both weighed 1/3000th of an ounce. Yet at maturity, there is a huge difference. The reason for the difference is that when the bonsai tree initially grows through the soil, the Japanese immediately tap its roots and in doing so, intentionally stunt its growth, resulting in a miniature tree.

On the other hand, the General Sherman had the benefit of unrestricted growth in the rich California soil, nourished by the minerals, rain and sun. The resulting giant is a magnificent specimen.

excerpt from Zig Ziglar, *See You at the Top*

If you supply the know-how and how-to's they will succeed and their growth potential is unlimited.

Whether your team is a bonsai tree or a General Sherman depends a whole lot on your ability to grow each team member. If you don't provide the necessary developmental nutrients, you will essentially stunt your subordinate's growth and they will fail. If you supply the know-how and how-tos, they will succeed and their growth potential is unlimited.

As the coach you are challenged to grow each team member to their maximum ability.

Why do we teach and train?

In the words of famous educator

Robert Mager:

*"We **teach** and **train** because we hope that through our **instruction,** students will somehow **be different** than they were before the instruction. We provide a **learning experience** with the intent that each student will be a **modified person** in **knowledge,** in **attitude,** in **belief** and in **skill."**

Most companies do provide some type of training. Some companies use their internal training departments while others use outside resources and still others expect the managers to do the training themselves.

Whatever system you use, remember: you are the coach and you are responsible for results. No matter how or under what circumstances the initial training occurs, it's your job to get the team to successfully apply what they learned. Many managers think that because the trainee has been to a training class, that's the end of it. That's only the beginning. Your job now is to make sure that what was learned is effectively applied out in the field.

> *No matter how or under what circumstances the initial training occurs, it's your job to get the team to successfully apply what they learned.*

It goes back to the old saying, "If you don't use it, you lose it." Do you think that coach Mike Shanahan of the Denver Broncos practices on Monday, takes the week off and says, "Okay it's game day, now let's go get 'em." I don't think so. Good coaches are in the trenches every day implementing strategies and teaching skills. Keep in mind that coaching is the daily pursuit of excellent performance. That doesn't happen with a one time event. In a nutshell, the acrostic "PROCESS" paints the developmental picture of training.

P-R-O-C-E-S-S

P – **Planning**. Planning provides for a strong training foundation. As the coach, you're on the front line. No one knows the external customers like you and no one knows the internal customer like you. This knowledge arms you with information that is important to all phases of the training program.

R – **Repetition**. I've stood in front of countless audiences asking the question, "After you have attended a one time training experience, how much do you think you retain?" We get answers ranging from 5 percent to 40 percent. The average response to the question is about 10 to 15 percent retention. If you're the coach of a business team, do you consider 10 percent retention good enough? The answer is an emphatic no! So how do you think you can improve retention and increase skills?

Skill development involves several steps. As we apply knowledge and practice a skill, we first become aware of what we don't know. That's the awareness step. We continue to practice even though we feel awkward. That's step two. We work through the awkwardness to become skilled. Step three. Eventually, with time and through repetition, what we do becomes a reflex. It's like being on auto pilot.

Skill Development Process

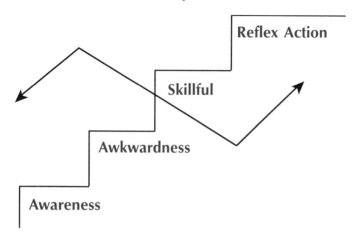

Reflex Action

Skillful

Awkwardness

Awareness

Depending on where you are on this development stairway, if you practice what you've learned, you become skilled. If you don't practice, you quickly lose your skills.

O – Ownership. As the coach, it is important that you take ownership for what is being taught to your people. If you do not believe in the training material and the system, then why should your people?

C – Content. The training content must be practical, pragmatic and relate to the real world challenges.

E – Evaluation. Only through evaluation and measurement can you identify where you are, know how far you've come, and effectively forecast where you are going.

S – Simulation. Simulation of real world situations prepares the student for real world situations. Role play, case studies and interactive discussion apply what is learned.

S – Support Material. One of the main reasons subordinates fail is because they lack the tools to get the job done. Tools that challenge thinking and promote action are important to the skill development process.

5. <u>FAIL TO MOTIVATE THEIR PEOPLE</u>

Through the decades, managers continue to ask the same question: "How do I motivate my people?" Some say you can motivate others. Some say you can't. The truth is, you can't motivate people because ultimately they can only motive themselves. You can inspire and you stimulate but you really don't motivate. Motivation is a motive, reason, or cause for action or inaction. It is the reason for the action or inaction.

Motivation is defined within the word itself. Break the word in half and it reads motivation (motive for action). It is the need, the desire, the want-to that results in a certain type of behavior. The **MOTIVATION** part of coaching is about shaping behavior and begins by understanding cause and effect. The effect is the actual observable behavior and the cause is the reason for the behavior.

> *Maybe the single most powerful principle of coaching is to understand that people are motivated for their reasons, not yours.*

Maybe the single most powerful principle of coaching is to understand that people are motivated for their reasons, not yours.

*The **motivation** part of coaching is about **shaping behavior** and begins by **understanding** **cause** and **effect**. The **effect** is the observable behavior and the **cause** is the **reason** for the **behavior.***

-5-

MOTIVATE
TO IMPROVE
PERFORMANCE

> **"You** *ou cannot push anyone up a ladder unless he is willing to climb it himself."*
> **Andrew Carnegie**

"You get the best effort not by lighting a fire beneath them, but by lighting a fire within them."

Bob Nelson
Motivational Specialist

What is your motivation strategy? Do you use the carrot? Do you use the stick?

The Stick — Fear Motivation

There's a funny story told about a rich Texan who throws a coming out party for his daughter. During the party, he offers the ranch or his daughter's hand in marriage to the man who can swim the length of the pool which is filled with alligators and crocodiles. Suddenly there is a big splash, and a boy swims the length of the pool unscathed. The rich Texan says to the boy, you have passed the test, and asked him whether he wants the ranch or his daughters' hand in marriage. The boy responds that he wants neither; he wants to know the name of the guy who pushed him into the pool.

The coach for the Australian swimming team must have heard the story, because that's how he is now attempting to motivate his swimmers. The coach starts the swimmers off, then releases a crocodile into their wake. Now that's fear motivation. We'll measure its effectiveness at the 2000 Olympic Games, if there is anybody left.

Fear motivation has been around since the beginning of time and I'll bet it will be around until the end of time. Managers use it at work, parents use it at home. It might be the most used type of motivation, even though it is the least effective. I say least effective because although it works, it is very short lived.

The use of fear, threats or intimidation as a motivation tactic usually ends in conflict, hostility and reduced productivity. Few managers claim to use it openly, but it is ever present in almost every company in America. Fear is sometimes used as punishment, but most often it comes in the form of threats, such as:

- Produce or else!
- It's my way or the highway.
- Get in or get out.

The industrial revolution mentality serves no one well, including the manager. The fear type of motivation often changes behavior and sometimes improves performance, but only for a short time until that person is able to find another job.

Carrot — Praise, Recognition, Rewards

Motivation must be intrinsic for it to work long term. It must be meaningful, so let's not exclude any type of program; let's just say that for motivation to be effective it must be meaningful to the person being motivated. That means you must really know your people so you can customize the motivation. One person on the team is motivated by affiliation, and thus may want a cash incentive program to buy the new car they've been want-

> **L**et's just say that for motivation to be effective it must be meaningful to the person being motivated.

ing. Some others may be motivated by power and will do anything to earn a promotion. Someone else may have a unique health situation that has impacted performance at work. They may need understanding and support. What I'm saying is that motivation is personal and it's internal. The good thing about employee motivation is that what motivates people most usually costs management the least. The beating heart of motivation is relationship development. It's the one on one relationship that managers have with every member of the team.

We have learned that behavior is shaped by consequence and recognition is a powerful consequence. Research tells us that open, two-way communication, personal caring, and effective leadership are some of the most important factors that employees look for in seeking employment. The old saying that "people don't care how much you know, they just want to know how much you care," is still alive and well today.

Recently, I received a phone call from one of my past employees that I had managed. He had moved out of state and was calling to catch up. Before he hung up, he reminded me of a card that I had written to him praising him for his work and accomplishments. He reminded me that he still has that card. Wow!

All motivational plans begin with relationship development, starting with praise, recognition and education. These elements are core to long term effectiveness.

MOTIVATIONAL PLAN

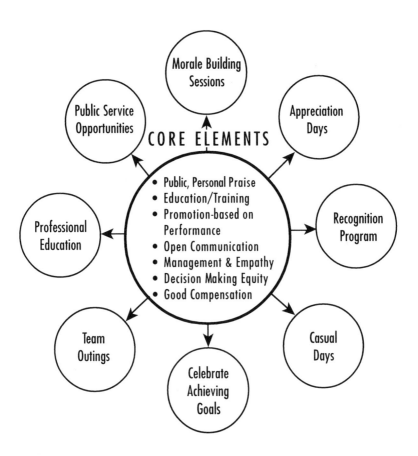

Praise and Recognition

One of the main reasons people leave their jobs is because managers fail to recognize and praise their people. Praise ranks higher than money, job titles or job security. People just want to know they are doing a good job and that they are appreciated for what they do. Employees ask themselves, "What is the point of going the extra mile if no one even knows the difference?" Never assume your subordinate feels appreciated. You've got to tell them. Sit down and just tell

> *E*mployees ask themselves, "What is the point of going the extra mile if no one even knows the difference?"

them how much you value their work. The rules for praising are to be sincere, be specific and be timely. Tell them what they did to deserve the praise. Tell them how it makes you feel and why it's important. Another powerful way to praise is to tell other people about an individual's accomplishments. This is especially powerful because it provides public recognition and can satisfy several needs at once.

Training and Development

Training and development are building blocks to achieve effectiveness and success. You may consider it a given in working with a company. Not so. Many companies throw people to the wolves with just **on the job training** (OJT). That's a piece of the puzzle but not near enough. Most employees expect to be trained. These are dollars well spent that will yield future dividends.

Promotion Based on Performance

Promotions should be based on ability and performance. Politics has no place in the promotion arena. A political placement can easily break up a team and seriously erode relationships. Create a promotion policy based on performance and interest, and live by it.

Open Communication

Those individuals who work face to face with the customers are in a unique position to add value to the company. They are on the front lines and they see and feel the impact of a change in the marketplace. Your success depends on the feedback you get from these scouts in the field. Never forget that knowledge flows from the bottom up. Take time to listen and to learn from your people.

Management Empathy

Empathy is the ability to put yourself in the shoes of another person and understand how they feel. It's difficult to separate the emotional, professional, physical and spiritual parts of the employee. You can't. You must work with the whole person and that means be empathetic to issues other than just job issues.

> **W**hy? Because if that person is not happy at home that behavior will affect their performance on the job.

Why? Because if that person is not happy at home, it likely will affect their performance on the job. Again, take time to let them know you care and to be flexible to the needs of your team.

> *If you want an* **employee** *to* **think** *like an* **owner** *and eventually assume* **responsibility** *like an owner, give them a* **voice** *in* **decision making** *that im-* **pacts** *their jobs.*

There is no better way to develop pride and ownership than to successfully implement employee ideas.

Compensation

Pay people what they are worth with a good base pay. In addition, provide the opportunity to earn more through incentives, bonuses and benefits. There are a few who live by the phrase, "Show me the money," but for the most part as long as the compensation is fair, money is not the main motivating factor for most employees. One underlying factor that connects all core elements of the plan is the emphasis that employees be shown that they are a valued company resource.

In addition to the core elements, companies must provide additional opportunities and program initiatives such as:

- Morale building sessions
- Monthly recognition programs for superior quality, sales and service
- Celebrating achievements such as projects and goals accomplished
- Providing professional education credit hours
- Public service opportunities
- Casual days
- Appreciation days
- Team outings

The challenge of motivation goes back to the understanding that we all have different needs and we all respond differently to different consequences.

*There is not one **cookie-cutter** approach to **motivation**. It's not a **mechanical process;** it's more like **chemistry** and it's as **personal** as one's DNA.*

-6-

COACHING
EVALUATION

.

COACHING EVALUATION

Indicate a rating of 1-10 on the following questions by writing the appropriate number in the blank. 1 = Poor, 10 = Strong

1. As a business leader and coach I effectively communicate the idea that everyone ultimately serves or sells the external customer. **Rating**
   1   2   3   4   5   6   7   8   9   10   _____

2. Everyone within my business unit clearly understands the company mission.
   1   2   3   4   5   6   7   8   9   10   _____

3. As a business leader and coach I work continuously to develop my people.
   1   2   3   4   5   6   7   8   9   10   _____

4. As a business leader and coach I possess a clear picture of my coaching philosophy.
   1   2   3   4   5   6   7   8   9   10   _____

5. All members of my business unit understand the part they play in fulfilling the mission.
   1   2   3   4   5   6   7   8   9   10   _____

6. The members of my business unit feel free to communicate new ideas and solutions regardless of how silly they sound.
   1   2   3   4   5   6   7   8   9   10   _____

7. Often an employee's success on the job is driven by personal needs off the job. Rate your awareness of what motivates your people.
   1   2   3   4   5   6   7   8   9   10   _____

8. Prior to interviewing a new applicant I always review the skills and qualities necessary to effectively perform the job.

1   2   3   4   5   6   7   8   9   10   _____

9. Within the last six months I have taken the time to review, create, or modify the job description for the different positions within my team.

1   2   3   4   5   6   7   8   9   10   _____

10. Prior to interviewing a new candidate I take time to review the interview process and prepare a detailed list of appropriate questions.

1   2   3   4   5   6   7   8   9   10   _____

11. As the business leader/coach I understand the importance of two-way communication.

1   2   3   4   5   6   7   8   9   10   _____

12. As the business leader/coach I regularly give and get feedback from the members of my team.

1   2   3   4   5   6   7   8   9   10   _____

13. As the leader/coach of my business unit I lead by example and demonstrate personal accountability.

1   2   3   4   5   6   7   8   9   10   _____

14. I effectively communicate that the practice of blame finding, procrastination, and making excuses have no place on the team.

1   2   3   4   5   6   7   8   9   10   _____

15. As the manager/coach I consistently execute the practice of problem giving as a method to develop my people.
1   2   3   4   5   6   7   8   9   10   _____

16. Members of my business unit practice personal accountability by always asking themselves, "How can I make a difference."
1   2   3   4   5   6   7   8   9   10   _____

17. I set and write quarterly personal and professional goals.
1   2   3   4   5   6   7   8   9   10   _____

18. As a leader/coach I effectively serve as a catalyst to help motivate my people.
1   2   3   4   5   6   7   8   9   10   _____

19. I use a structural praise process to reinforce belief in my subordinates.
1   2   3   4   5   6   7   8   9   10   _____

20. I regularly give meaningful "pats on the back" to express my thanks and appreciation.
1   2   3   4   5   6   7   8   9   10   _____

21. I take time each day to find subordinates doing things right and often write short notes of appreciation.
1   2   3   4   5   6   7   8   9   10   _____

22. To effectively coach my business unit and I take time to understand and respond to the different needs of my subordinates.
1   2   3   4   5   6   7   8   9   10   _____

23. I often ask the opinion of subordinates and encourage decision making equity.
    1   2   3   4   5   6   7   8   9   10   _____

24. Everyone in my business unit is aware of and understands the standards of their job.
    1   2   3   4   5   6   7   8   9   10   _____

25. As the coach I teach skills and processes and explain the reasons behind using these skills and processes.
    1   2   3   4   5   6   7   8   9   10   _____

Now total your score: _____

SCORES:

0-150	Call Excellence in Action Partners NOW! 1-888-505-9052
151-186	Below standard. Focus on areas of weakness.
187-225	Meets standard. You are an effective and productive coach.
226-250	Excellent! You are an outstanding, highly productive coach.

Chick Waddell, managing partner of Excellence in Action Partners is an internationally known speaker, teacher, and corporate coach. Chick is a business growth specialist and has worked in the areas of sales, management and motivation for over 14 years. He has served as Master Trainer and Account Executive for the Fortune Group International and Zig Ziglar Corporation. He has also been the Director for National Accounts for one of the largest health care companies in America.

He has authored several articles and books including *Sales Coaching Playbook, Play by Play Selling, Coaching to Win* and the *Business Development Tool Kit.*

PRODUCTS AND SERVICES

Books and Resources

 *Sales Coaching Playbook* – A sales coaching system created to increase performance, productivity and profitability. 205 pages $14.95

 *Play by Play Selling* – A guide to help sales professionals successfully plan and conduct productive sales calls.
$7.95
Also made available on the Internet at www.ITI4Training.com

 *Coaching to WIN*
A manager's guide to developing people to achieve results.
$7.95

Seminars and Keynotes (Sales, Management, Motivation)

Call and schedule Chick Waddell for your next management conference or keynote speech.
Speeches 45-90 minutes

Seminars and Workshops 1/2 day–3 days or as requested by client.

For Additional Information call:
1-888-505-9052
www.chickwaddell.com

Yes, please send me extra copies of
Coaching to Win.

Quantity	1-99	100-199	200-999	1000-4,999	5,000+
Price Each	$7.95	$6.95	$6.35	$5.95	$5.50

Coaching to Win _____ copies x $ _____ = $ _____

Shipping and Handling $ _____

Subtotal $ _____

Sales Tax (7.75% – **Texas Only**) $ _____

TOTAL (U.S. Dollars Only) $ _____

Handling Charges

Total $ Amount	Up to $99	$100-249	$250-1199	$1200-$3000	$3000+
Charge	$8	$12	$25	$65	$100

Name _____ Job Title _____

Organization _____ Phone _____

Shipping Address _____ Fax _____

Billing Address _____ E-mail _____

City _____ State _____ Zip _____

❑ Please invoice (Orders over $200).
Purchase Order Number (if applicable): _____
Charge your order:
      ❑ MasterCard ❑ Visa ❑ American Express ❑ Discovery

Credit Card Number _____ Exp. Date _____

Signature _____

❑ Check or Money Order enclosed payable to Excellence in Action Partners.
❑ I am interested in learning more about Excellence in Action Partners
❑ I am interested in having Chick Waddell speak at a corporate function.

FAX: 866-505-9052

MAIL: 356 Parkview Place, Coppell, TX 75019

WEB: www.chickwaddell.com

PHONE: 888-505-9052